Dr. Jaerock Lee
Junior Bible Study

Foreword

God Created the World with Love

Do you think a clock is able to suddenly just come into existence from parts? Did the sun appear to start rising every morning and the moon start shining at night in such orderly fashion by chance?

As all things in the world are made by someone, there is nothing including the heavens, the earth and all things in them that just happens to exist by coincidence. The God of love designed them with clear purposes and then He created them (Romans 1:20).

Why did God create this world and form a man?

Before the beginning of time, God existed all by Himself. He was filling up the whole original universe in the form of original light that contained sound. At a certain point of time He came to think, 'How happy I feel if I have someone who knows My heart and with whom I can share love.' As He made a plan for human cultivation, He divided the original universe, where He existed all by Himself, into the spiritual world and the physical world. He also came to exist as God the Trinity, took on the form of a man, and started the work of the Creation.

As the appointed time came, God the Trinity came down to the earth that was covered with the water of life. He established the foundation for people to live just as parents decorate the room for their baby that is on the way. On the first day, He surrounded the earth with the original light that brings about the works of Creation and He separated light from darkness.

On the second day He made expanse. On the third day He created the ground, the sea, and vegetation. On the fourth day He set the sun, the moon, and stars. On the fifth day He caused the waters to team with creatures and put birds in the sky. Then, on the sixth day He first made all the living creatures upon the land.

It was after He prepared the environment for humans that on the sixth day, God finally formed man in the image of God. He Himself made all organs and cells with His powerful hands and He put His hope in that creation. He wanted humans to look towards God the Creator and see the beauty of all creatures with two eyes. He wanted them to praise God with lips, and to listen to God and obey His Word with ears.

After He created the first man Adam, He planted the Garden of Eden and placed him in it. God taught him spiritual knowledge and blessed him to enjoy authority and blessings given as God's child. On the seventh day, God rested on the earth that He had created with love while hoping that countless children would come forth through human cultivation.

Now, let's travel through the seven-day providence in which God performed amazing works of the Creation with His original light and voice!

Table of Contents

Foreword
The Bible at a Glance

1 God the Creator
Evidence of God's Creation — 8

2 The Creation of the Earth
The Earth Created with Love — 16

3 The First Day of Creation
The Creation of Light — 24

4 The Second Day of Creation
The Creation of the Expanse (Heaven) — 32

5 The Third Day of Creation
The Creation of the Earth, Seas, and Vegetation — 40

6 The Fourth Day of Creation
The Creation of the Sun, the Moon, and Stars — 48

7 The Fifth Day of Creation
The Creation of Living Creatures in the Waters and Birds — 56

8 The Sixth Day of Creation (1)
The Creation of Cattle, Creeping Things, and Beasts — 64

9 The Sixth Day of Creation (2)
The Creation of Human Beings — 72

10 The Seventh Day of Creation
God's Rest and the Sabbath Day — 80

The Mysteries of Creation

★ More than 60 Trillion Cells /
The Amazing Length of the Circulatory System   14

★ Skin Is Renewed Every Month /
The Nose and Bronchial Tubes Working as Air Cleaners   22

★ The Mucus Membrane Protects the Stomach Wall /
Each Nostril Takes Its Turn Smelling   30

★ The Reason Solid Ice Is Lighter Than Liquid Water /
Hexagonal Water, Hexagonal Snow Crystals   38

★ Hexagonal Beehives and Dragonfly's Ommatidia /
The Woodpecker's Shock Absorber   46

★ A Spider Web Is Stronger than Iron /
Ants Use the Sunlight   54

★ Ants' Way to Survive /
A Biological Sonar System of Bats and Dolphins   62

★ Principles of Shark Scales /
Mussels, Material for Biobinding Agent   70

★ Camels' Secrets to Surviving /
Birds' Instinct in Building Houses   78

★ Plants with Self-protecting Ability /
Creatures' Homing Instinct   86

Appendices   Summary of Creation
The Confession of God the Creator
God Is Truly Alive!

The Bible at a Glance

Mysteries of the Beginning

Creation of Spiritual and Fleshly Worlds

Adam and Eve in the Garden of Eden

God the Origin

He existed in the form of light that contains sound

original light | original voice

God the Trinity

4th heaven: God's dwelling place
3rd heaven: the heavenly kingdom
2nd heaven: Eden and the area of darkness
1st heaven: the Earth

↓

Angels and cherubim
Celestial bodies except for our galaxy
An unstable Earth at the early stage

The Beginning (John 1:1)
"In the beginning was the Word…"

Lucifer's rebellion and failure

The beginning (Genesis 1:1)
"In the beginning God created the heavens and the earth."

Extinction of dinosaurs, pet of a living being Adam

Construction of three pyramids and the Sphinx near the Nile

The original light cohered, resulting in the division of spirit and heavens

7-day Providence

First Day

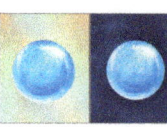

Light and Darkness

Second Day

The Expanse (heaven)

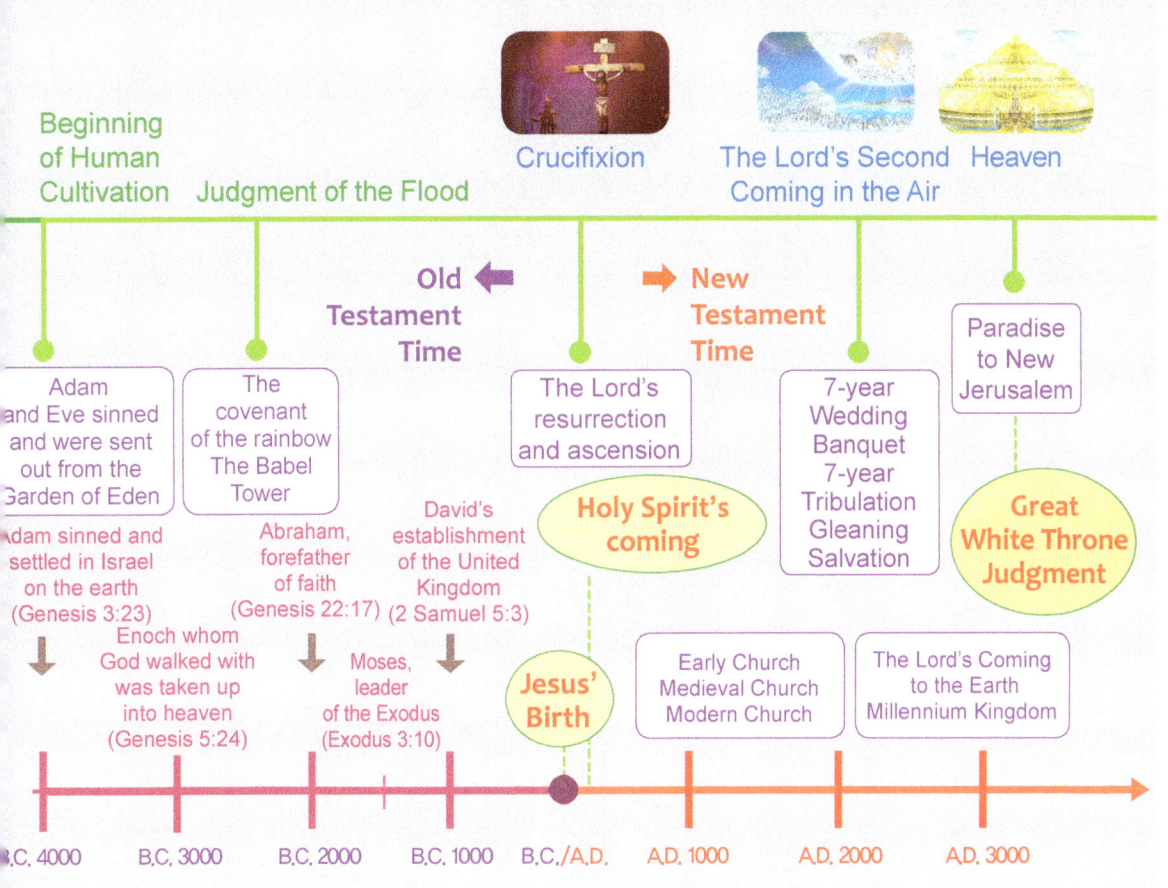

"But do not let this one fact escape your notice, beloved, that with the Lord one day is like a thousand years, and a thousand years like one day" (2 Peter 3:8).

Third Day	Fourth day	Fifth day	Sixth day	Seventh day
Land, Sea, and Vegetation	Sun, Moon, and Stars	Living Creatures in the Water and Birds in the Sky	Living Creatures on the Earth and Human beings	God's Rest

Chapter 1

God the Creator
Evidence of God's Creation

Reading

"In the beginning God created the heavens and the earth" (Genesis 1:1).

More on the Word

"For since the creation of the world His invisible attributes, His eternal power and divine nature, have been clearly seen, being understood through what has been made, so that they are without excuse" (Romans 1:20).

Suppose one day the parts of an airplane were blown up into the air.
As the parts later dropped, they regrouped, came together
and again became an airplane! Can you believe it?

Living beings are incomparably more complex than a plane.
How likely is it that a living being could
come into existence at random by chance?
It is completely impossible.

1 God the Origin Planned 'Human Cultivation'

Before the beginning of time, God had existed in the original universe all by Himself. He was filling up the whole original universe in the form of light that contained sound (John 1:1; 1 John 1:5).

God had existed alone for an eternity of years and at some point He came to have a thought. He planned to gain another being who could feel everything mysterious in the universe and who could share love together with Him forever in the beautiful Heaven. To have such true children, He planned 'human cultivation'.

A farmer sows the seeds, reaps the wheat, and gathers them in his barn. In the same way, God made a plan to create men, cultivate them, and bring them into Heaven.

The Form of Light That Contained the Original Voice in the Beginning

2 The Truth of Creation and the Falsehood of Evolution

Everything from the smallest screw to a complete airplane is made by someone. Nothing can just happen to exist. There is nothing in the heavens or on the earth that has come into existence by coincidence. God the Creator designed everything with a specific purpose and intention. Many people, however, do not know that God created all things. They do not believe it, either. Why?

Most schools teach evolutional theory. The Creation of God is not taught. Evolutionists claim that life emerges from non-living matter, and that lower organisms evolve into higher organisms and breeding of the same species results in evolving of broader classes of species. Does it, really?

Scientific developments have shown the evidence evolutionists have presented is false. For example, some evolutionists argued that a man evolved from ***an ape** that looks like a monkey. They presented fossils of some skeletons, teeth, and arm and leg bones as the evidence of intermediate stage of evolution. However, it was later revealed that they are not the fossils of the intermediate stage, but they are fossils of orangutans, extinct species of pigs, and monkeys.

 3 Evidence of the Creation

There are numerous people on the earth. They have varied appearances and they have different skin colors. But regardless of their races they all have two eyes, two ears, a nose, and a mouth. Their locations are the same in all people as well. This also applies to every kind of animal including an animal living in the mountains, a bird flying in the sky, or a fish in the sea. Their facial structure is almost the same although each species may have its own unique characteristics.

Additionally, everything in the solar system such as the earth's revolution and

rotation, the ebb and flow of the tide, the movement of wind and forming of clouds all work in an orderly manner. This is the evidence of God who created and governs the earth, and all things on the earth.

What if the earth's period of rotation were lengthened? The daily temperature range would be so large between day and night that life could not exist on the earth. If the earth and the sun were farther apart we could not live on the earth because it would be very cold. If they were closer, we could not survive the heat.

What about the location of the moon? The moon must be

in its current location. The *gravitation between the moon and the earth enables the earth to rotate securely and life to survive on the earth.

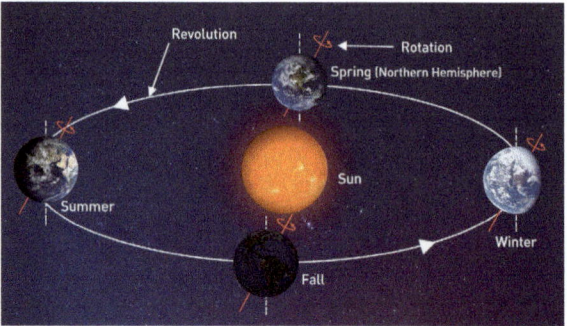

Rotation and Revolution of the Earth

What would happen if the moon were farther than it is now from the earth or the moon disappeared? The gravitational pull would not be able to securely support the earth's axis of rotation. Then, the earth would rock and shake like a top right before it stops spinning.

Ebb and Flow of the Tides

Was it by accident that all these things came to operate in such an orderly manner? No, it wasn't. All things in the universe were created by God the Creator, and He made all of them suitable for human existence.

| An Ape | Apes include chimpanzees, gorillas, orangutans, and other animals in the same family. |
| Gravitation | In physics, gravitation is the force of attraction between two objects due to mass. |

1. Here is the explanation of God the Origin. Fill in the circles.

   In the beginning God the Origin filled up the whole original universe in the form of ◯◯◯◯◯ tthat contained ◯◯◯◯.

   God planned human cultivation to gain ◯◯◯◯ ◯◯◯◯◯◯◯ with whom He can share love forever in the beautiful Heaven.

2. Here is the summary of the reading above.
   If it agrees with the information given in the reading, write TRUE. If not, write FALSE.

   ❶ Most people learn about Creation in school. (　　)
   ❷ There are many evidences of the Creation in heavens, the earth, and all things in them. (　　)
   ❸ All things in the universe were created for a clear purpose. (　　)
   ❹ There are high chances that living organism is created by accident. (　　)

3. Write about the evidences that God created heavens, the earth, and all things in them.

13

Mystery of Creation

More Than Sixty Trillion Cells, The Genetic Information Stored in the DNA Is 1,000-encyclopedia-volume Worth!

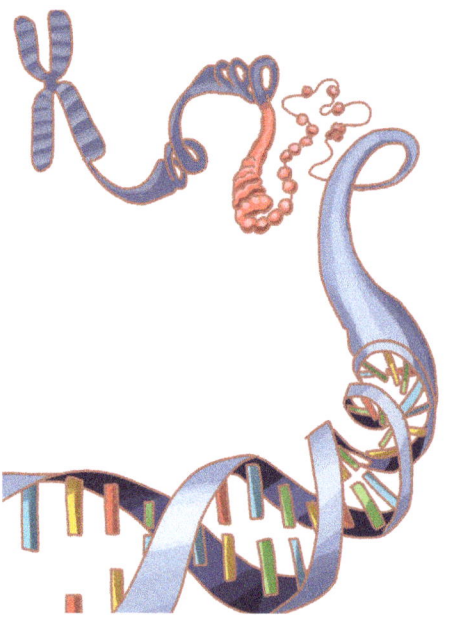

Human body consists of sixty trillion cells, which is an unimaginably big number.

God put all genetic information of each man into the DNA of the nucleus. Facial appearance, height, physical structure, and skin color, plus all kinds of information about body organs and their functions are stored in such a tiny nucleus.

The diameter of a nucleus is about 5 micrometers; 0.0005 centimeters. We cannot even see it with the naked eye. What if we tried to write on paper all the DNA genetic information stored in such a tiny nucleus?

The paper will become 1,000 encyclopedia volumes with 1,000 pages each. All this huge amount of information is stored in such a tiny part as a nucleus. Isn't it amazing?

There Are Enough Blood Vessels That Their Combined Length Can Go Around the Earth Three Times, But It Takes Blood Only 46 Seconds to Circulate throughout the Whole Body!

There are many thick and thin blood vessels in our body.

How long would it be if we connect all of them?
It would be approximately a hundred twenty thousand kilometers.
This is the length that can surround the earth three times.

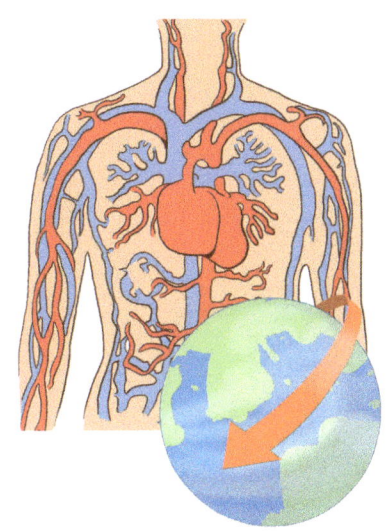

How much blood do you think pass through the heart for a minute?
It is around five liters, and this blood from the heart travels every corner of our body and it takes just about 46 seconds. It means blood circulates in the whole body more than a thousand times per day.

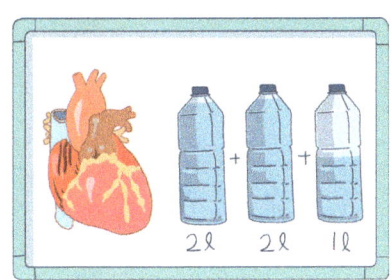

Chapter 2

The Creation of the Earth

The Earth Created with Love

Reading

"The earth was formless and void, and darkness was over the surface of the deep, and the Spirit of God was moving over the surface of the waters" (Genesis 1:2).

More on the Word

"And, 'You, LORD, in the beginning laid the foundation of the earth, and the heavens are the works of Your hands'" (Hebrews 1:10).

Before swimming

Before playing tennis

Before playing soccer

What do you have to do?

You have to do warm-up exercises.
Preparation is very important in everything.
God also made preparations in advance
before He created the earth.

1. The Earth Created before the Sun, the Moon, and Stars

God the Origin planned human cultivation, and at some point He came to exist in the form of God the Father, God the Son, and God the Holy Spirit. At that time, there was already the earth in the first heaven.

The first earth that God created in the fleshly space

When the earth was created, there was no sun, no moon, and no stars in this galaxy. It hung in the space by the power of God. The first earth God created did not look as it now looks. The crust and atmosphere of the earth were unstable. Referring to this unstable status of the earth, the Bible says, "The earth was formless and void."

2. The Reasons God Did Not Create the Earth Perfectly from the Beginning

The first reason was because God followed the natural law of the physical world.

Although God is almighty, He did not ignore the physical order and followed the natural process. The first heaven, where the earth is located, is the physical space, and thus He created the earth according to the order of the physical world.

Even when we build a small house, the work of laying its foundation and putting up its frameworks is a must. We cannot build a complete house from the beginning overnight. This is the order of the physical world.

When God created the earth, He started with laying its foundation according to the physical order. He went through many steps of combining elements that formed the earth and making the earth's ***crust** and ***atmosphere** in balance. Through the process of laying its foundation, the earth came to have the land and the air; the proper environment for human beings.

The second reason was because He loves us.

Since this earth is the place for His children to live in, God had a perfect blueprint and created it over a long period of time with earnest desire. He did not create it overnight but He laid the foundation of the earth, created heavens, and filled the earth with all the necessary things. He did all with love.

God harbored the whole earth and created it just as parents decorate a room and prepare necessary things with earnest longing for a child who is soon to be born.

3 God Covered the Earth with the Water of Life

In laying the foundation of the earth, God Himself came down to the earth. He intended to make the most appropriate environment for humans and all living things to live. Back then, the earth was covered completely with water.

God moved over the earth covered with waters, and the Bible expresses His actions saying that "The Spirit of God was moving over the surface of the waters."

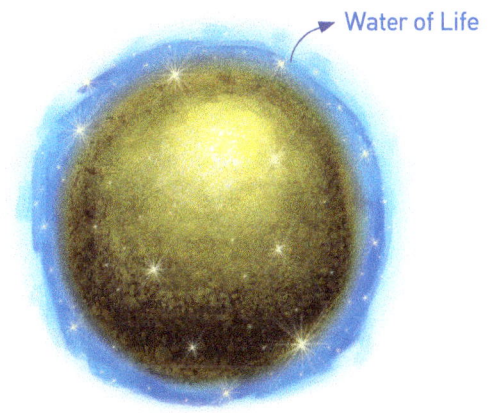

Water of Life

Then, where did the water that covered the entire earth come from? It was the water of life that flowed from the throne of God.

The water of life that originates from the throne of God flows through New Jerusalem to Paradise. It then returns back to the throne of God. It was this water of life that God covered the earth with when He created

 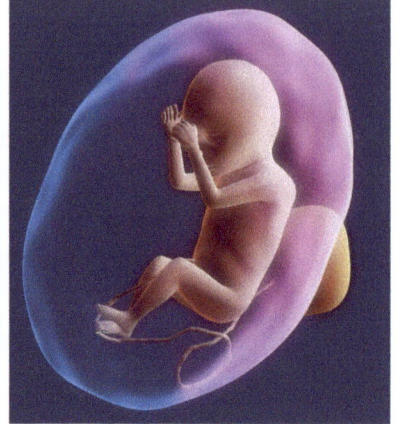

the earth. He put the water of life as well on earth which is the fleshly world as He put it in the spiritual realm.

 4 The Reason God Covered the Earth with the Water of Life

The earth, when it was covered with the water of life, looked like a baby kept in amniotic fluid in its mother's body. While covered with this amniotic fluid, the baby is provided with nutrients from its mother through the umbilical cord until it comes to have a complete look of a man. Thanks to this amniotic fluid that covers the baby, the baby can be protected from any external shocks or infections. The fluid also helps to keep the body temperature of the baby constant. While the earth was in the water of life just as a baby in the amniotic fluid, it came to be life-filled and waited for the first day of Creation.

| Crust | The outer layer surrounding the surface of the earth |
| Atmosphere | The layer of air or other gases around the earth |

1. The first earth used to be unstable. Why did God not create the earth perfectly from the beginning? Fill in the blanks.

   The first reason was to follow the _____ of the _____ world.

   Second, because He _____ us.

2. Write TRUE if the following sentences agree with the information given. If not, write FALSE.

   ❶ Although the earth in the first heaven is located within the physical world, God laid its foundation according to the spiritual law. (   )
   ❷ God created the earth overnight. (   )
   ❸ God laid the foundation of the earth and created heavens over a long period of time with earnest. (   )
   ❹ The earth was created first before the sun, the moon, and stars in the galaxy were created. (   )

3. Where did the water that covered the earth come from? Fill in the blanks.

   The _____ of _____ flowing from the _____ of God

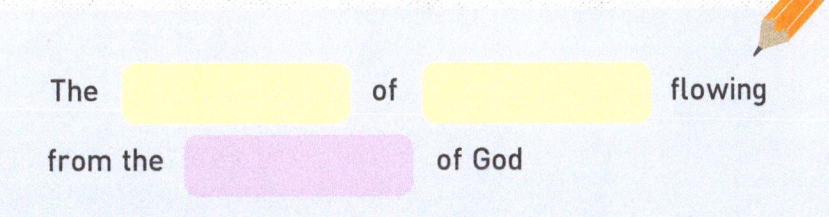

Mystery of Creation

Human Skin Is Renewed Every Month!
Human Bone Is Four Times Stronger than Concrete!

Human skin constantly peels off and renews; it is completely renewed every 4 weeks. It is as though you put on a new natural water resistant suit of skin every month and around 1,000 times in one's lifetime.

An adult has 206 bones, and they have amazing power.

A bone which is half the size of the palm of your hand can support 10 tons. In fact, it is stronger than concrete. It is four times stronger than concrete that is used to build a house.

approximate weight of 100 big adults that weigh 100kg

300 to 500 Million Alveoli in the Lung, The Nose and Bronchial Tube Working as the Air Cleaner!

A lung is like an energy reservoir that provides body with oxygen. Each lung has about 300 to 500 million alveoli, which are suspended like grapes. If stretched out, it would be an area that is about half the size of a basketball court.

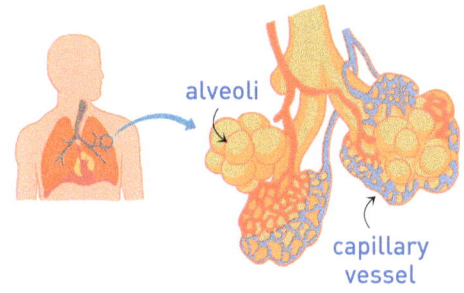

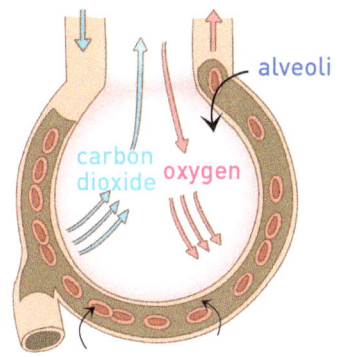

Alveoli are designed to be surrounded densely by capillary vessels so that the exchange of oxygen and carbon dioxide is effective.

Air passes through your nose and bronchial tubes before going into the lungs. They work like air cleaners.
The air is cleaned moving through the nose and goes to larynx and into bronchial tubes.

The bronchial tubes have many cilia (short thread-like projections), and mucus (thick liquid) that is secreted, which filters out dust and germs. The dust and germs come out through sneezing and coughing. Through this process, it sends as clean air as possible to lungs.

Chapter 3

The First Day of Creation
The Creation of Light

Reading

"Then God said, 'Let there be light'; and there was light. God saw that the light was good; and God separated the light from the darkness. God called the light day, and the darkness He called night and there was evening and there was morning, one day" (Genesis 1:3-5).

More on the Word

"This is the message we have heard from Him and announce to you, that God is Light, and in Him there is no darkness at all" (1 John 1:5).

The fastest fish
Sailfish
(110 to 128km/h)

The fastest bird
Frigate bird
(400 to 418km/h)

The fastest land animal
Cheetah
(80 to 120km/h)

There is one element that is incomparably far faster than all of them.

It is light.

Light can travel around the earth seven and a half times in a second.

 **God Surrounded the Universe that the Earth Belonged to with the Original Light**

On the first day of the Creation, God first said, "Let there be light." Then, the universe where the earth belonged was surrounded by the light. What kind of light was this? Was it the sunlight? Since there was no sun yet at that time, it was not the sunlight.

This light was the original light. Since the power and authority of God is contained in this original light, something can be created from nothing in the light. That is why God surrounded the earth with the original light and started the work of the Creation.

The original light covered the universe that the earth belongs to

 **What Happened When the Earth Was Surrounded by the Original Light?**

First, order and principles were established in the fleshly space. For example, rules were set up like "The earth shall rotate once a day, and revolve around the sun once a year", "Water flows from higher to lower", and "Water freezes at 0 Celsius degree and boils at 100." Not only the order and principles of the earth, but other orders and principles governing the sun, the moon, other planets, and countless stars to be created were also set up on this first day.

Next, God's power and divine nature were put into all creation. God's power can bring the dead back to life and make living organism grow well. When you sow a seed in the ground, it sprouts and grows up. For a seed to sprout and bear fruit, it needs proper ground, water, and sunlight. Since God's power and His divine nature is put into the ground, water, and sunlight, a form of life can sprout.

The light that was put into the ***creatures** still remains, and it works as fundamental energy that holds all the living things.

3 God Separated the Light from the Darkness

When God covered the fleshly space with the original light and separated the light from the darkness, there were day and night. Even from the first day when there was no sun, how could day and night be separated? The answer is in the original light. While there was the original light covering the earth, it was day. When it was withdrawn, it was night.

The present earth which we live on rotates once a day. The side where the earth faces the sun as the earth rotates is "day", and the other side where it doesn't face the sun is "night." It is the sun that separates day from night now. However, on the first day of the Creation, it was not the sun that separated day from night because there was no sun.

The earth when there was original light (Day)

The earth when the light was withdrawn (Night)

4. What Is the Spiritual Meaning of "God Separated the Light from the Darkness"?

It means God divided and separated the domain of light that belongs to God from the domain of darkness that belongs to Lucifer. As it was the first night, God released Lucifer and evil spirits from the ***Abyss.**

Just as there were day and night on the earth, God who is the Light, allowed the evil spirits to have authority to manage the world of darkness. Of course, the evil spirits can employ their authority only within the boundary that God permitted.

As day and night can never coexist with each other, never can light and darkness as well. Thus, children of God, who is the Light, must cast off darkness and walk in the Light (Ephesians 5:8). In other words, we must keep and act upon the Word of God. Evil spirits cannot touch those who walk in the Light.

Creatures	All things God the Creator created
Abyss	The deepest place of Hell

1. According to Genesis 1:3, God said, "Let there be light" and there was light. What kind of light was it?

   [   ]

2. Fill in the blanks with the words below.

   > things, creatures, hope, thanks, nothing,
   > power, divine nature, authority, God

   ❶ The _____ and _____ of God are contained in this original light. _____ can be created from _____ in the original light of Creation.

   ❷ When God surrounded the earth with the original light, _____'s power and _____ were put into all the _____.

3. Write TRUE if the following sentences agree with the information given. If not, write FALSE.

   ❶ The sun separated day from night on the first day. (   )
   ❷ When God covered the earth with the original light, the light separated day from night. (   )
   ❸ Evil spirits received the equal authority with God the Creator. (   )
   ❹ God allowed evil spirits to manage the world of darkness. (   )

Mystery of Creation

Gastric Acid Is Strong Enough to Dissolve Zinc! The Mucus Membrane Protects the Stomach Wall!

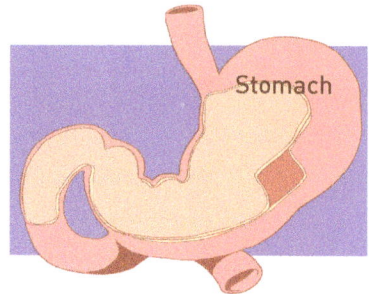
Stomach

Food goes into the mouth, passes through the esophagus and arrives at the stomach. Then, the stomach secretes gastric acid and it makes the food a thick liquid-like porridge and absorbs nutrients.

The gastric acid includes an enzyme called pepsin which splits proteins in the digestion of food.
It also kills germs that are harmful to human body.
However, this gastric acid has such a high level of acidity that it can dissolve zinc. So, at times it may damage the stomach. To protect itself, the stomach secretes mucin from its wall.

The gastric acid is secreted regularly at breakfast, lunchtime, and dinner time. That is why the stomach may have a problem when you eat irregularly or overeat.

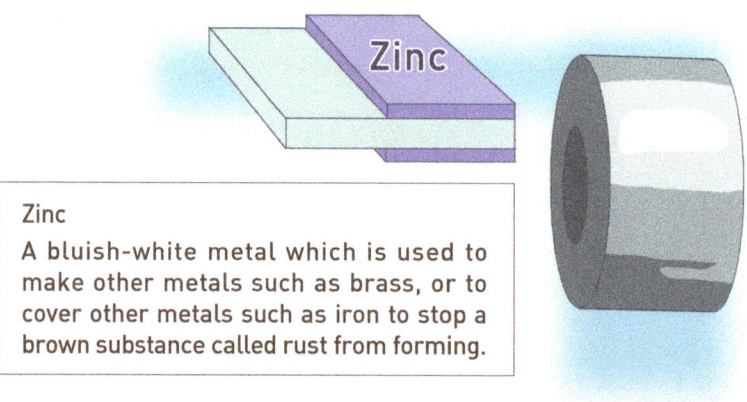

Zinc
A bluish-white metal which is used to make other metals such as brass, or to cover other metals such as iron to stop a brown substance called rust from forming.

The Eyes Blink 900 Times an Hour!
Each Nostril Takes Its Turn Smelling Every 3 or 4 Hours!

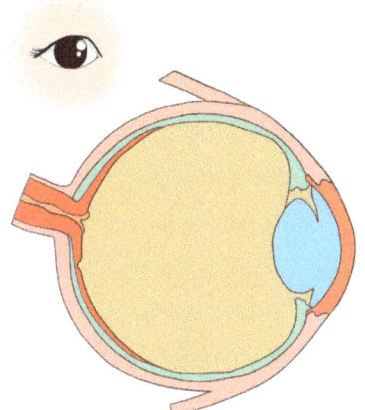

It takes less than one second for man to blink the eye once.
It actually takes 1/40 of a second!

The blinking of the eye protects the eye, and soothes and lubricates the cornea.
The eyelid protects the pupil by quickly coming down when dust enters into the eye.

What about the nose? Every 3 or 4 hours, the two nostrils take turns smelling.
One nostril detects odors and the other just passes the air waiting its turn to smell.

The ears have eardrums that receive sound vibration. In the eardrum a certain substance is produced that smells very bad. This is to prevent any tiny insects or worms from entering. If they enter, they come back out from the ears because of the bad smell.

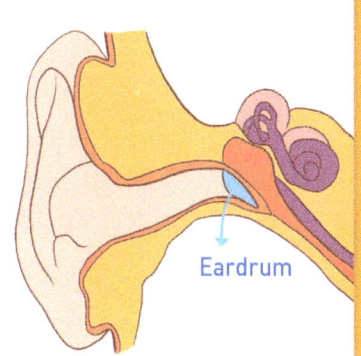

Eardrum

Chapter 4

The Second Day of Creation
The Creation of the Expanse (Heaven)

Reading

"Then God said, 'Let there be an expanse in the midst of the waters, and let it separate the waters from the waters.' God made the expanse, and separated the waters which were below the expanse from the waters which were above the expanse; and it was so. God called the expanse heaven. And there was evening and there was morning, a second day" (Genesis 1:6-8).

More on the Word

"For He draws up the drops of water, they distill rain from the mist, which the clouds pour down, they drip upon man abundantly" (Job 36:27-28).

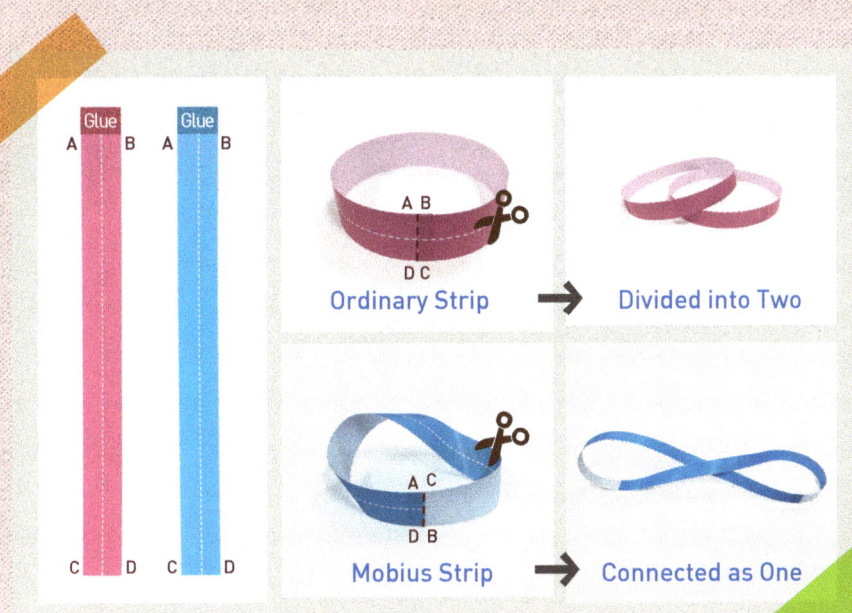

You can take a strip of paper and make a
Mobius band by giving it a half twist.
You cannot distinguish inside from outside.
If you cut it following the dotted line,
it won't be divided into two. Isn't it amazing?

There are many interesting things on the earth.
So, should there not be even more
in the spiritual world!

1 What Is the Expanse God Created?

On the second day of the Creation, the earth was still submerged in the water of life. God then said, "Let there be an expanse in the midst of the waters, and let it separate the waters from the waters."

The expanse refers to 'heaven', i.e. the atmosphere which covers the earth.

The atmosphere is the layer of air from the ground up to at an altitude of about 1,000 kilometers. The atmosphere performs many important functions. There is oxygen in the atmosphere that is necessary for humans and animals to breathe and carbon dioxide for plants. In addition, the atmosphere absorbs harmful rays of light that come from the sun or from the outer space. It also plays the role of a shield that helps to protect the earth's surface from the impact of meteorites.

It also absorbs and holds some of the heat from the surface of the earth to keep the earth warm. It also reduces the temperature difference in parts of the earth by dispersing the heat evenly through *convection and *advection currents. Thanks to all these, living things can survive on the earth.

2 The Waters above the Expanse and the Waters below the Expanse

After God created an expanse, He divided the waters that covered the earth into the waters above the expanse and the waters below the expanse.

The waters below the expanse was the water left on the earth. This water gathered and became the sea on the third day. The water above the expanse was moved into the second heaven which is the spiritual world and became the source of the rivers in Eden (Genesis 2:10-14).

Later after God created Adam and led him to the Garden of Eden, the waters (above the expanse) poured upon the four areas of the earth and formed four great rivers. These four rivers are in relation to three of the four major ancient civilizations. The first river, the Pishon, is related to the Indus civilization. The second river, the Gihon, is associated with the Egyptian civilization. And, the third and fourth rivers, the Hiddekel and the Euphrates are associated with the Mesopotamian civilization.

 When the Expanse Was Created, What Happened in the Spiritual World?

When the expanse was made, the sky was given in the first heaven, and the second heaven was divided into two parts; the domain of light that belongs to God and that of darkness that belongs to evil spirits.

In the domain of light, there are the Garden of Eden where the first man, Adam, lived and the venue of Seven-year Wedding Banquet where the saved children will meet the Lord their Bridegroom.

Then what is there in the domain of darkness? This is the place for Lucifer, who betrayed God, and evil spirits that followed Lucifer.

4. The Reason the Bible Does Not Say "It Was Good" on the Day God Created the Expanse

For five of the six days of the Creation, the Bible says, "…and God saw that it was good." But it is only on the second day of the Creation that this expression is not found. What is the reason? The reason is that the domain of darkness where the evil spirits dwell was created in the expanse on the second day.

Then why did the God of love make this domain of darkness? It is to achieve human cultivation in justice. Because there are evil spirits, people experience darkness and come to long for light. Just as those who experienced sickness know the importance of health so well, by experiencing darkness they can also realize how good the light and truth are.

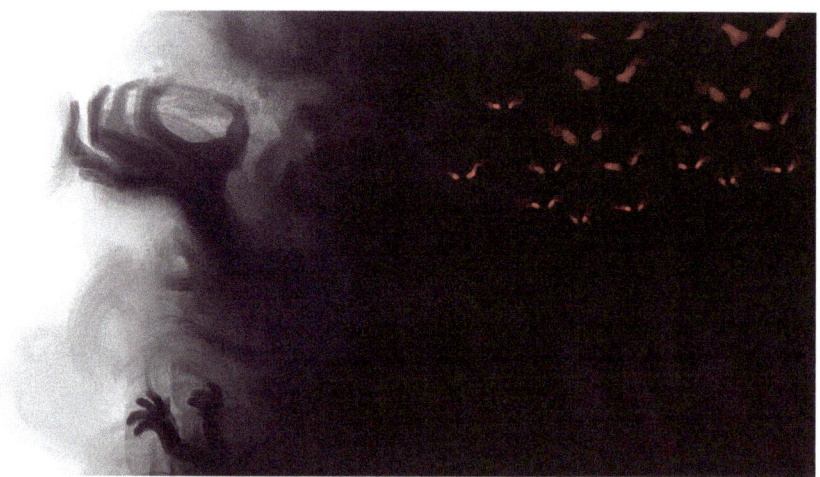

Convection	The process by which heat, water, other gases and liquids move upward (vertically) in the atmosphere
Advection	The lateral or horizontal transfer of heat, water, other gases and liquids in the atmosphere

1. What did God create on the second day? The initial letters are given.

In the first heaven:	e_____ (atmosphere)
In the second heaven:	the domains of l_____ and d_____

2. What do the waters above the expanse and the waters below the expanse each refer to? Match them.

   The waters below the expanse •   • The source of rivers in Eden

   The waters above the expanse •   • The water left on the earth became the sea

3. The Bible does not say "it was good" to God's eyes only on the second day. Why is it?

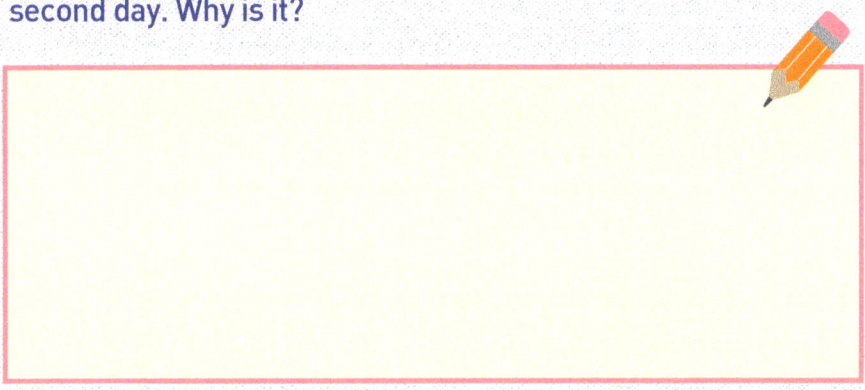

Mystery of Creation

The Reason Solid Ice Is Lighter Than Liquid Water

Ice is hard and solid but it is lighter than water because the density of ice is lower than that of water. Here is the providence of the Creation.

There are living things in the cold sea waters such as the seas in Polar Regions. They can live because ice floats over the surface of water. The ice blocks coldness from the outside, and the water temperature can be maintained.

If ice were heavier than water, the surface of the sea would freeze becoming ice and then the ice would sink. Eventually this would cause all water to become frozen to ice.

Hexagonal Water, Hexagonal Snow Crystals

In the grandeur of nature, many proofs of God's design and Creation can be found. Among them, certain regular and well-organized figure-like (geometric) forms are found. One of the typical examples is the hexagon.

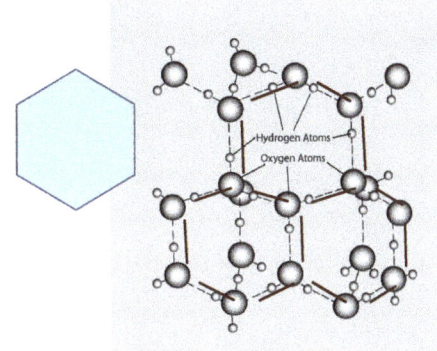

The molecule binding of water, that is the most beneficial for human body, is in the form of a hexagon. Water with this form is called "hexagonal water". Research studies verify that when a body is comprised of hexagonal water the cells are the most active and have greater ability to deal with diseases.

Though snow crystals are all different from each other, amazingly their basic shapes are all the same! The shape is that of the hexagon. No matter how superiorly skillful and talented a designer may be, he cannot make so many varied and beautiful designs with only one basic geometric shape as the hexagon!

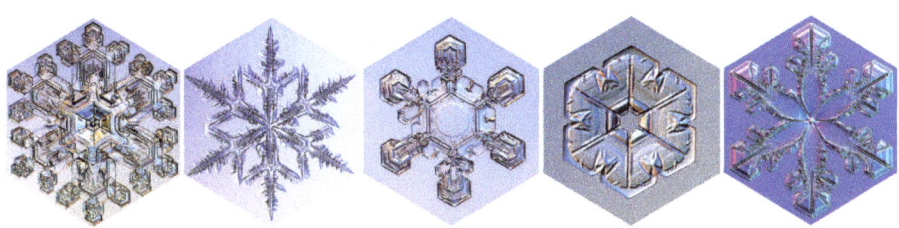

Chapter 5

The Third Day of Creation
The Creation of the Earth, Seas, and Vegetation

Reading

"Then God said, 'Let the waters below the heavens be gathered into one place, and let the dry land appear'; and it was so. God called the dry land earth, and the gathering of the waters He called seas; and God saw that it was good. Then God said, 'Let the earth sprout vegetation, plants yielding seed, and fruit trees on the earth bearing fruit after their kind with seed in them'; and it was so. The earth brought forth vegetation, plants yielding seed after their kind, and trees bearing fruit with seed in them, after their kind; and God saw that it was good. There was evening and there was morning, a third day" (Genesis 1:9-13).

More on the Word

"Behold, I am the LORD, the God of all flesh; is anything too difficult for Me?" (Jeremiah 32:27)

dandelion seeds → parachutes

maple tree seeds → propellers

The flight of a dandelion seed in the wind
was modeled after in the making of parachutes.
The falling of a maple tree's seed
which draws a circle was modeled after in inventing
the propeller for the helicopter.

These plants, which are equipped
with wonderful devices for flying,
were all created by God the Creator.

1 How Were the Earth and Seas Created?

On the third day of the Creation, the entire surface of the earth was almost flat with no high mountains or deep valleys. It was this kind of earth with such flat ground and covered with the water of life. Then, God gave out the original voice, saying, "Let the waters below the heavens be gathered into one place, and let the dry land appear." Then, ***crustal movements** took place.

A huge hole formed near the North Pole, waters gathered into it, and it became "the sea".

The land was revealed at the South Pole

At this time God caused a huge hole to form near the North Pole. As there came to be a huge hole, the waters covering the earth gathered in the North Pole. As the North Pole sank, in equal reaction, the South Pole rose up. God called the waters, "the seas" and the dry land revealed at the South Pole, "earth." The evidence is that North Pole and South Pole both are covered with glaciers but they are different. Under the glaciers in the North Pole is the sea while under the glaciers in the South Pole is the land. On the third day, the seas were gathered into one, and there was only one continent. On the fourth day, the earth took a form similar to that of the current earth, i.e. the five oceans and the six continents, came into existence through crustal movements known as Plate Tectonics.

2 The Reason God Made the Seawater Salty

The waters that covered the earth gathered together to become seas. Now, when did the seawater become salty? Was the water of life that covered the earth salty? Not at all! As God called the gathered waters "the seas," God made them contain salt, and they became 'salty'. What is the reason that God made the seawater salty?

First, it is to keep the waters of the seas from corrupting. Through common sense we know that flowing water like that of rivers doesn't stagnate and that it is the stagnant water that pollutes and decays. The seawaters are stagnant waters contained in a huge vessel called "the earth". Thus, chances are that the seawaters may decay over time. By putting salt in it, God prevented microorganism from growing and the waters from decaying.

The second is that it can greatly benefit the life of man. Salt from the sea is a necessity for man. Most of all, salt plays an important role inside the body of humans and animals to maintain life. It is also used to season food, or to salt food to preserve it. God knew that salt is a must for human beings to exist, and He arranged for it to be dissolved into the sea waters.

As the seas and earth were made, the Bible says, "God saw that it was good." Just as parents are happy to prepare necessary things for their beloved baby, God was happy after He made necessary things for us on the earth.

 3 All Kinds of Plants Created on the Earth

After He created the earth and the seas, God created all kinds of plants. All kinds of plants and vegetation and trees were made. Generally, it takes years for a fruit tree to bear fruit. However, it was done instantly on the third day of the Creation. At the word of God, the roots were extended under the ground, trunks and branches grew up and flowers bloomed and fruit were yielded immediately.

Since plants cannot move, God gave them the ability to survive. He gave them the seeds containing life and let them propagate seeds. He even gave them the ability to spread their seeds in diverse and effective ways.

4 Why Did God Create Plants ahead of the Sun?

You may have a question here. On the third day, there was no sun. But God created plants that can survive only when there is sunlight. What is the reason God made plants before He created the sun? It is to show all the things in the universe are under the power of God! (Ref: Jeremiah 32:27)

That is, by creating plants ahead of the sun, God revealed that the fundamental power to maintain all things in the universe is in the hand of God. The same applies to Heaven. There is no sun in the heavenly kingdom, but there is no darkness because of the light of God's glory. The power of light enables flowers and trees to live forever without withering.

| Crustal movement (Plate Tectonics) | Movement resulting from or causing deformation of the earth's crust like the land rising up or sinking of land |

1. Here is the summary of the reading above. Write TRUE if the following sentences agree with the information given. If not, write FALSE.

   ❶ After crustal movement, waters gathered at the South Pole. (   )
   ❷ When God called the gathered waters "seas", the waters became salty. (   )
   ❸ On the third day, there was one landmass and one sea. (   )
   ❹ Every kind of plant on the earth took root and bore fruit in an instant. (   )
   ❺ On the third day, since there was no sun, the plants withered. (   )

2. Why did God put salt in the sea water and make it salty?

★ First, _____ the sea water

★ Second, _____
   for our life's need of salt

3. God urged us to become light and salt in the world. What do we have to do to become light and salt of the world?

Mystery of Creation

Hexagonal Beehives and Dragonfly's Ommatidia (Compound Eye)

Have you seen the hive that honey bees construct?
The hive has the structure of many hexagons regularly adjoined to each other. The structure has no gaps between the hexagons.

The wall of this hexagonal hive is 0.1 millimeter thick. With this thin wall, it can store honey which can be 30 times heavier than the hive itself.

What does the eye of a dragonfly look like?

A dragonfly has a pair of compound eyes each of which consists of countless hexagonal ommatidium. Each ommatidium looks in different directions. Thus, without turning its head, a dragonfly can see broadly and is well aware of objects' movements at the same time.

Scientists studied the eyes of dragonflies and invented endoscopes which can sense minute changes inside a human body and cameras which can take pictures of movements with 360 view angle.

The Shock Absorber of a Woodpecker That Drills Fifteen Times a Second

A woodpecker can drill at a tree fifteen times a second.
It pecks a hole on the tree with its beak and eats worms with its long tongue.

A woodpecker can balance itself with its hook-like claws and strong tail feather so it can hang on the tree for a long time. When it drills at a hard tree fifteen times a second, how strong is the physical impact?

When a rocket launches, the astronaut is influenced greatly by gravitation because of the high speed. The physical impact a woodpecker experiences is 250 times stronger than the astronaut has in the rocket. If an ordinary bird pecked at the tree, it would die from cerebral concussion!

For a woodpecker, God created a special shock absorber between its beak and skull so that the impact can be absorbed.

Chapter 6

The Fourth Day of Creation
The Creation of the Sun, the Moon, and Stars

Reading

"Then God said, 'Let there be lights in the expanse of the heavens to separate the day from the night, and let them be for signs and for seasons and for days and years; and let them be for lights in the expanse of the heavens to give light on the earth'; and it was so. God made the two great lights, the greater light to govern the day, and the lesser light to govern the night; He made the stars also. God placed them in the expanse of the heavens to give light on the earth, and to govern the day and the night, and to separate the light from the darkness; and God saw that it was good. There was evening and there was morning, a fourth day" (Genesis 1:14-19).

More on the Word

"Then Jesus again spoke to them, saying, 'I am the Light of the world; he who follows Me will not walk in the darkness, but will have the Light of life'" (John 8:12).

Gears in a clock mesh with each other
at an exact speed and tell us the time.

Planets in the solar system and countless stars move
at exactly the right speed on a precise track
according to natural laws established by God.

 **God Created the Sun, the Moon, and Stars around the Earth**

On the fourth day of the Creation, God said, "Let there be lights in the expanse of the heavens to separate the day from the night." What does it mean?

From the first day to the third day of the Creation, when God surrounded the earth with the original light, it was day, and when God withdrew the light it was the night. However, after God created the sun, the moon, and stars on the fourth day, the earth began to rotate on its axis once a day and to revolve around the sun once a year, which established the cycle of days and years respectively.

As the earth rotates, on the surface of the earth that faces the sun it was the day, and on the other part it was the night. The day and night now automatically began to change.

The sun, the moon, and stars were created with the earth as the center

 **Signs Appeared after the Sun, the Moon, and Stars Were Created**

After God created the sun, the moon, and stars, He said, "Let them be for signs and for seasons and for days and years." As He said, many signs appeared on the

earth. The first was atmospheric phenomena.

When the sun was created and its light reached the surface of the earth, the water of the seas produced water vapor which rose into the sky to form clouds. The differences resulting from the amount of the heat of the sun on the earth's surface caused differences in temperatures. These thermal differences caused the winds to blow. Due to the work of clouds and winds that carried them, it rained or snowed in different places of the earth. Then, rivers and lakes were formed on the lands, and plants were provided with necessary water.

Next, seasons, days, and years were established. The earth is tilted by 23.5 degrees while revolving around the sun. As a location on the earth's surface gets close to the sun, the intensity of the sunlight increases and warms the area. On the other hand, a place farther from the sun receives less intense sunlight and the place is cooler. This results in the seasonal cycle of spring, summer, fall, and winter.

Spring

Summer

Fall

Winter

As the earth began rotating and revolving, the concept of 'a day' and 'a year' came to an existence. The time that it takes for the earth to rotate once is 'a day', and that it takes to revolve around the sun once is 'a year.'

3 The Spiritual Meanings in the Sun, the Moon, and Stars

The sun gives bright light to us and is the source of all the energy that is necessary for every living thing on earth. It is essential in our lives. As 1 John

1:5 says, God is Light and in Him there is no darkness at all. Just as mankind cannot live without the sun's physical light, we cannot live apart from God who is spiritual Light. That is, we must all dwell in the Word of God who is Light.

What is the spiritual meaning contained in the Creation of the moon and stars? The sunlight during the day and the moonlight and starlight during the night lighten up darkness. As there is light both during the day and night, the light of the truth of God shines over all the places all the time.

Not only when we experience times of joy and happiness, but also when we are confronted with difficult situations that are like the darkness of night, we should remember that God is Light and He is with us. This is the spiritual reason God created the moon and stars in the dark night sky.

The sun is the source of light and energy provided for all living things

The moon and stars lighten up darkness at night

1. Tell the day from night. Fill in the blanks.

From the 1st to 3rd Day	Day or Night	From the 4th day
The time the earth was surrounded with ( )	Day	the place that faces the sun
The time ( ) was withdrawn	Night	the place that turns its back on the sun

2. Check how much you dwell in the Word of God who is the Light.

Check Points	O	△	X
I pray during the prayer meeting without hanging out with friends.			
I read a chapter of the Bible a day.			
I listen attentively to the message during the worship service.			
I do not argue or fight with my siblings or friends.			
I obey the words of my parents.			

3. Why did God let the moon and stars shine in the dark night sky? Let's talk about its spiritual meaning.

Mystery of Creation

A Spider Web Is Stronger than Iron, and the Spider Produces a Variety of Silk for Different Purposes

A spider catches its prey with thin threads in the air. The spider's web seems fragile, but it is five times stronger than iron cord of the same thickness. It can support something that weighs 4,000 times more than a spider. A web that is 1 millimeter thick is capable of supporting a full grown man.

A spider discharges liquid protein in its body through its back and produces thin silk thread. Thread is produced for a variety of purposes—for example, for protecting its eggs, wrapping its prey, connecting other threads or objects, etc.

In addition, the web is as soft as silk, and it has excellent elasticity. And it ventilates well, but water cannot pass through it, so that these characteristics are used to produce body armor or parachute material.

Ants Look for Different Food Depending on Necessary Nutrients, and Take Its Course Relying on the Sun

On the earth are more than 10,000 different kinds of ants. Some may think ants are just small insects but more than 95% of the 10,000 kinds are beneficial for men.

Scientists showed an interesting finding through studies on ants' ecology. Ants look for their food based on their needs of nutrients. For instance, when they have many actively growing larvae, ants collect food which is full of protein that is a necessary nutrient for larvae. When they have many worker ants, they collect food which is full of carbohydrates that is the energy producer.

Most ants secrete 'pheromone' and find the way by remembering its smell. They also find their direction to go by using the sun. That is, it seems as if they remember the angle between them and the sun to return home.

Chapter 7

The Fifth Day of Creation
The Creation of Living Creatures in the Waters and Birds

Reading

"Then God said, 'Let the waters teem with swarms of living creatures, and let birds fly above the earth in the open expanse of the heavens.' God created the great sea monsters and every living creature that moves, with which the waters swarmed after their kind, and every winged bird after its kind; and God saw that it was good. God blessed them, saying, 'Be fruitful and multiply, and fill the waters in the seas, and let birds multiply on the earth.' There was evening and there was morning, a fifth day" (Genesis 1:20-23).

More on the Word

"Look at the birds of the air, that they do not sow, nor reap nor gather into barns, and yet your heavenly Father feeds them. Are you not worth much more than they?" (Matthew 6:26)

Most saltwater fish in the ocean cannot live in
freshwater such as rivers or lakes.
On the other hand, freshwater fish cannot live
in the seawater that contains salt.

Then, how would you explain this aquarium
where **freshwater and seawater fish
coexist together?**

1. "Let the Waters Teem with Swarms of Living Creatures"

On the fourth day of the Creation, clouds and winds were formed, and it began to rain in various places. It created rivers, lakes, and brooks and streams. The remnant water was absorbed into the land and held under the land and it became underground water.

God let the land have waters that are necessary for all living things to exist. After all proper environments were set in place for all living things to live, on the fifth day God said, "Let the waters teem with swarms of living creatures."

At this time, fish were created not just in the sea waters, but also in the fresh waters. The shellfish with hard shells; mollusks such as squid and octopus; bottom-creeping things under the seas such as crabs and crawfish; plankton that floats in the ocean, and underwater plants were also created on this day.

2. What Do the 'Great Sea Monsters' Refer to?

They refer to fish which are immense in size such as whales. Currently, the largest whale existing on the earth is the blue whale. Blue whales reach up to 33 meters in length.

Although whales live in the water they are not fish, but mammals. Unlike other fish, whales don't lay eggs, but give birth to live young. They nurse their calves with milk and they breathe air through pulmonary respiration. Isn't it amazing?

God specially created the whale, which is one of the great 'monsters,' in order to destroy theories of evolution.

Evolutionists argue that living things evolve in the order of: fish, amphibians, reptiles, birds, and mammals. If they were right, their theories could not explain the reason whales, which are mammalian and the most evolved species in the order, live in the waters like fish do. The reason is simple; God created them that way.

Evolutionists do not want to believe it. They claim that whales in waters evolved to be able to live both in the waters and the land, and then they evolved more to live on the land over a long period of time. They further claim such nonsense that whales evolved to go back to the waters since they starved on the land.

What would have had to happen to whales, which live in the waters, to be able to live on the land? The fins would have disappeared and legs would have had to develop for walking instead of fins for swimming. It is nonsense. But they even insist that their legs that they had developed over a long period of time, disappeared and again, the fins reformed, and then they went back into the sea! Does it make sense? No, not at all. It is impossible even with a long period of time. This single case tells us much about the falsehood of evolutionism.

3 "Let Birds Fly above the Earth in the Open Expanse of the Heavens"

On the fifth day God created birds that fly in the sky after their kind as well as various living creatures in the waters. If you take a close look at birds, you can find that birds are specially constructed so that they can fly in the air. Unlike other animals, birds have many bones that are hollow and their lungs have air sacs, so that they can fly in the sky well.

As explained, it is not that living creatures in waters and all kinds of birds flying in the sky evolved to fit in the environment. God designed and created them from the beginning after their kind. He gave them abilities to survive in a given environment. So, good-hearted people acknowledge God just by seeing the nature of things and all things in it and believe Him who created them.

1. God said, "Let the waters teem with swarms of living creatures". What do "the waters" refer to? Choose all.

   ❶ Lakes ❷ Crystal sea in Heaven ❸ Brooks and streams

   ❹ Rivers ❺ Tap water ❻ Sea

2. Circle all living creatures in the waters.

3. God gave fish and birds various abilities to survive depending on their environments. Then, what abilities did God give you?

Mystery of Creation

Ants' Way to Survive

Leafcutter ants cut leaves into pieces, bring them home, and pile them up. Then, fungus grows from the pile of leaf pieces, and these ants use the fungus as food. Aphid-herding ants "milk" the aphids to make them excrete a sugary honey dew-like substance and feed on it.

If ants find food, they work together to carry it. At first, a couple of ants try to take it. But when they find it is beyond the scope of their strength, they quickly call for other ants. Then, dozens or even hundreds of ants team up to take the food home.

Generally, an ant can carry 50 times its own body weight. As ants move in the unity as one in a perfect order, although no one forces them to do, they can enjoy tremendous strength. Even large animals cannot survive when attacked by a swarming group of ants.

A Biological Sonar System of Bats and Dolphins

It is pitch dark deep in waters so nothing is seen.
Submarine navigation uses sonar to figure out the location of objects out there around it.

This navigation system was developed in 1990s, but there are animals that have used this technique since a very long time ago. They are bats and dolphins.

They make ultrasound and wait for sound to bounce back. With the sound, they perceive obstacles and prey.

The fossil of a bat that existed 50 million years ago does not look different from bats of today.
It shows that they already used the 'high-tech' biological sonar system even 50 million years ago.

Chapter 8

The Sixth Day of Creation (Part 1)
The Creation of Cattle, Creeping Things, and Beasts

Reading

"Then God said, 'Let the earth bring forth living creatures after their kind: cattle and creeping things and beasts of the earth after their kind'; and it was so. God made the beasts of the earth after their kind, and the cattle after their kind, and everything that creeps on the ground after its kind; and God saw that it was good" (Genesis 1:24-25).

More on the Word

"Because the foolishness of God is wiser than men, and the weakness of God is stronger than men" (1 Corinthians 1:25).

Leafcutter ants grew mushrooms before mankind.

Polyergus samurai ants make use of the tactics used in the army.

Odontomachus ants can exert strength that is 300 times more than their own weight.

God gave ants such abilities to survive
although they look weak.

Then, how much more does God want to
fulfill the hearts' desires of His loving children?

1 God Created Living Creatures of the Land after Their Kind

On the sixth day of the Creation, God created living creatures of the land after their kind. What do 'cattle' refer to? They include livestock kept by men such as cows, horses, sheep, and dogs. 'Creeping things on the ground' refer to reptiles, such as snakes, crocodiles, and turtles; but they also include insects that creep and crawl on the ground, like ants. The 'beasts of the earth' simply refer to wild animals that people cannot easily tame such as lions, tigers, and leopards. Here, it is outstanding that from the beginning God separated those that are the 'cattle' which people can easily domesticate from those that are the 'beasts of the earth' that are not easily tamed.

Cattle refer to animals that are easily tamed by people

2 Why Did God Separate Cattle from Beasts of the Earth?

God knew what animals would be a necessity to people in the future. Surely, cattle also lived in the wild in the beginning. After Adam and Eve sinned, they came down to the earth and gave birth to their children. Then they began to keep cattle.

Initially, they caught animals in the wild and kept them in their houses. There were some animals which they could easily tame, but there were also others which could not be easily tamed. For example, animals like cows, horses, sheep, and dogs were easy to domesticate. On the other hand, wild beasts like tigers, lions, and leopards were difficult. It was because God created cattle which could do good for people in the future, and separated them from others from the beginning.

For human cultivation, God considered such a delicate part of the plan as this

Beasts of the earth refer to wild animals

while carrying out the works of the Creation.

 ## 3 What Did Living Creatures of the Earth Eat?

Before Adam committed a sin, the animals on the earth ate only grasses and drank water. The land of the earth was cursed when Adam and Eve disobeyed and ate from the tree of the knowledge of good and evil, and animals changed. They did not hurt or kill other animals but they lived in peace eating fresh grass given by God (Genesis 1:30). No animals were evil.

 ## 4 The Reason God Saw That It Was Good

As the land animals were created on the sixth day, everything that was environmentally necessary for human cultivation was finally set. God saw that it was good (Genesis 1:25). He rejoiced like a mother does when she finished preparing everything for a baby to be born.

Animals lived in peace and ate only grass and drank only water before the first man, Adam, sinned

When a woman conceives her baby, she may prepare many things even before the baby is born. She may prepare baby clothes, bedding, and toys and she is excited just to look at them. How happy and joyful do you think God felt as He made the environment perfect for human cultivation? And, with this thrill and excitement He finally created a man in His image.

1. Here are living creatures created on the sixth day. Match them up.

   Cattle • • Livestock • • snakes, crocodiles, turtles, etc.

   Beasts of the earth • • Reptiles • • lions, tigers, leopards, etc.

   Creeping things on the earth • • Wild animals • • grasshoppers, ants, etc.

   • Insects • • cows, horses, pigs, sheep, hens, dogs, etc.

2. Write TRUE if the following sentences agree with the information given. If not, write FALSE.

   ❶ God separated cattle from wild animals because He knew which animals would be necessary for people. (   )
   ❷ Both cattle and wild animals are easily tamed. (   )
   ❸ Before Adam committed a sin, all animals were not evil and they lived in peace. (   )

3. With excitement and thrill, God created the earth just like parents make preparations for their baby to be born.
   Let's confess our thanks for His love.

Mystery of Creation

A Full Body Swimsuit to Which Principles of a Shark's Scales Are Applied!

There are many kinds of sharks in the sea including saw sharks, shark suckers, sturgeon and so on. Some sharks can swim at a speed of 80 kilometers per hour. That is that they can move in the seawater as fast as 80 kilometers per hour. Isn't it amazing?

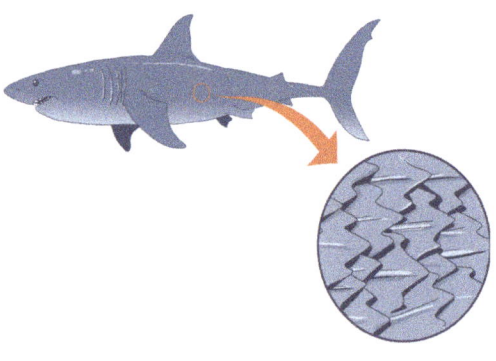

The scales of such a high-speed shark are equipped with a small device protruding on the body that reduces the frictional resistance (the power that pushes against the water in the direction opposite of forward motion).

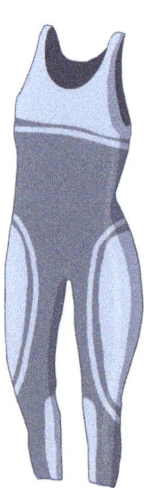

People have studied animals' and plants' unique and amazing abilities and applied them to cutting edge technologies. This kind of study is called 'biomimetics'.

There is a 'full body swimsuit' to which principles of a shark's scales are applied. A full body swimming suit has 10-15% less frictional resistance than a normal swimsuit. The swimmers wearing this full body swimming suit won 25 out of 33 gold medals in the Sydney Olympic Games 2000. It proved its efficiency.

Mussels Are Material for Biobinding Agent! Abalone Shell's Structure Was Used to Invent Tank Armor!

Mussels are known to have strong adhesive protein.
This protein enables mussels to stick to rocks under the sea water although a big wave comes.
The adhesive protein that mussels have is stronger yet more flexible than any other man-made adhesive.
When compared to man's tendon, it is 5 times stronger, and it stretches 16 times longer.

Since the adhesive protein of mussels is natural, it is safe for the human body, and thus it can be used as medical adhesive to adjoin torn skin or broken bones. Since this adhesive maintains its strength in water, it can be very useful to construct ships or battleships.

The shell of an abalone is very hard. Even if a truck ran over it, it would not break.
An American research team used the abalone shell structure to invent tank armor.

Chapter 9

The Sixth Day of Creation (Part 2)
The Creation of Human Beings

Reading

"Then God said, 'Let Us make man in Our image, according to Our likeness; and let them rule over the fish of the sea and over the birds of the sky and over the cattle and over all the earth, and over every creeping thing that creeps on the earth.' God created man in His own image, in the image of God He created him; male and female He created them. God blessed them; and God said to them, 'Be fruitful and multiply, and fill the earth, and subdue it; and rule over the fish of the sea and over the birds of the sky and over every living thing that moves on the earth'" (Genesis 1:26-28).

More on the Word

"The people whom I formed for Myself will declare My praise" (Isaiah 43:21).

An elephant eats about 185kg (400+ lbs.) a day (six 30kg-bales)

A brachiosaurus ate about 2.4 tons a day (eighty 30kg-bales)

What would have happened to plants and animals on the earth if dinosaurs had lived on the earth for 160 million years as scientists have argued? When were dinosaurs created, and why did they become extinct?

God explained the secrets about the Creation through the extinction of dinosaurs.

Creation of Dinosaurs

Falsehood of the Evolution of Dinosaurs

The Extinction of Dinosaurs

www.gcntv.org

1 God Created Man in His Own Image

On the sixth day of the Creation God created the first man Adam on the earth. He made Adam Himself in His image of dust from the ground along with the water of life. During the process, the original light that contains His infinite power and wisdom continually came into the man from the hands of God.

God breathed into Adam's nostrils the breath of life, and he became a living being. The breath of life is the fundamental power of God. Adam had milky white skin. His hair was golden blonde and reached the nape of his neck. He was around 175 centimeters tall (just over 6ft 4in). He was magnificent from head to toe.

The first man, Adam was created as a living being

2 Why Did God Form Man of Dust from the Ground?

Depending on what is added to the ground, the characteristics of the soil can change. Even if the field is good, if polluted water or soil is added to it, it becomes a bad field. On the contrary, even if the field is bad, as a farmer adds good soil, applies fertilizer, and diligently cultivates it, it eventually becomes a good field.

The same applies to human beings. According to what we accept in our freewill, our heart-field will become either a good heart or an evil heart. To the extent that you see, hear, feel, and practice what pleases God, you will become more good-hearted.

When He created man, God wanted to share true love with mankind. That is why God formed man from dust of the ground and gave him freewill. In other words, He created men in such a way that they can choose to love and trust God by themselves.

 ## 3   God Created Pets and Woman in the Garden of Eden

After creating the living being Adam, God planted a garden in Eden in the second heaven and there He placed the man whom He had formed (Genesis 2:7-8). God allowed him to govern and manage the Garden of Eden. He also allowed him to eat freely from any tree of the garden with one exception. He told Adam, "From the tree of the knowledge of good and evil you shall not eat, for in the day that you eat from it you will surely die" (Genesis 2:16-17).

God formed every beast of the field as well as every bird of the sky in the Garden of Eden. In addition to the kinds of animals God formed on the earth, in Eden He also created special kinds of animals that pleased Adam. They were dinosaurs and flying dinosaurs like the pterodactyl. Lastly, God caused a deep sleep to fall upon the man, and He took one of his ribs and formed it into a woman. He brought her to him as a helper suitable for him (Genesis 2:18-25).

Dinosaurs were created as Adam's pet in the Garden of Eden

 ## 4   After Creating Man and Woman, God Blessed Them

On the sixth day, after He created the man and woman, God blessed them (Genesis 1:28). First, He blessed them to "be fruitful and multiply, and fill the earth".

It was because Adam and Eve had to multiply by having many children for human cultivation. From among them many of God's true children could come forth through human cultivation. So, Adam fathered many children and enjoyed authority and blessings given by God for an immeasurably long period of time.

The second blessing was to "subdue the earth." The earth in this verse refers to not only this Earth in the first heaven, but also the Garden of Eden in the second heaven. While he was living in the Garden of Eden, Adam could freely come to the Earth. He also built three pyramids that symbolize God the Trinity and a sphinx near the beautiful Nile. It was to glorify God.

The third blessing was to "rule over the fish of the sea and over the birds of the sky and over the cattle and over all the earth, and over every creeping thing that creeps on the earth." As a result, Adam was even able to feel the emotions of animals due to amazing God-given wisdom and power to govern over them. He enjoyed the authority of the lord of all creation.

God created heavens, the earth, and all things in them for six days and He formed Adam and Eve and blessed them on the sixth day, and God rejoiced very much (Genesis 1:31). It was because He hoped with faith that countless people would come forth as His true children whom He can share love with through human cultivation. So then, when was the starting point of human cultivation to gain God's true children?

While living in the Garden of Eden, Adam and Eve lacked nothing. After a very long time had passed by, Adam and Eve failed to keep in their minds God's command telling him not to eat from the tree of the knowledge of good and evil. Eventually, they ate from the tree. Consequently, their spirits that work as the master of human beings, died just as God said, "For in the day that you eat from it you will surely die." They could no longer communicate with God who is spirit nor live in the Garden of Eden that belongs to the second heaven (Genesis 3:1-19).

After this happened, God made garments of skin for Adam and clothed him. And He sent him out from the Garden of Eden. Finally, he came to cultivate the ground from which he was taken. It was the beginning of human cultivation, which is to cultivate their heart-fields (Genesis 3:21-23).

1. God formed Adam of dust from the ground, and with His original power God let him become alive and move. What do we call that power? (Fill in the circles with appropriate letters.)

   The B ○ ○ ○ ○ ○ of ○ ○ F ○

2. Write TRUE if the following sentences agree with the information given. If not, write FALSE.

   ❶ God wanted to gain true children with whom He can share true love. (   )
   ❷ Man's heart and dust have something in common in which their attributes can change depending on what is added to them. (   )
   ❸ A man's heart can never become good-hearted as long as it is stained with untruth. (   )
   ❹ God allowed Adam to eat from all trees of the Garden of Eden including the tree of the knowledge of good and evil. (   )

3. Now let's discuss attributes of untruthful hearts that we should cast away to become God's true children.

❶ Hot-temper (Anger)	❹ Lying, deceiving heart	❼ Adulterous mind
❷ Ill-feeling (discomfort and bad-feeling)	❺ Judgment	❽ Greed, selfish-motives, covetousness
❸ Hatred, jealousy, envy	❻ Changing heart	❾ Betrayal

77

Mystery of Creation

Camels' Secrets to Surviving in the Hot Desert!

Camels' long eyelashes and thick eyelid form a barrier against a fierce wind of desert sand and protect their eyes.
Their thick coats protect them from scorching sunshine during the day and freezing coldness of the night.

They chew the cud all day. This is one of the ways they can survive in the hot desert.
By chewing the cud of food and water, they can live in the desert without eating for days.

Camels can store 100 to 150 liters in their stomachs, which help them walk in the desert without drinking any water for 8 to 10 days.
They can also travel 95 to 120 kilometers a day even with 500kg-loads on their back.

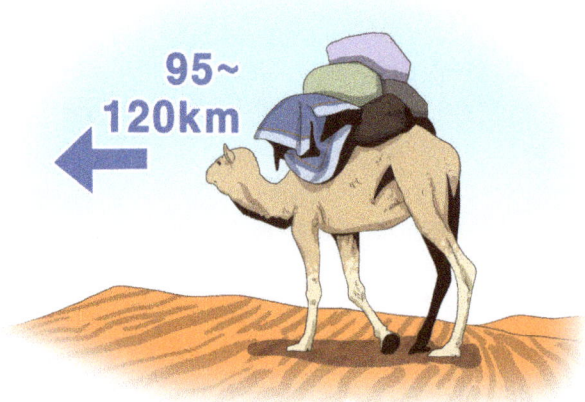

Birds' Building Houses by God-given Instinct!

Birds make a nest for their babies. Some make it with soil and straw, and some others with grass and leaves. Tailorbirds in India even build it by pecking leaves, making holes on them, and sewing them.

A biologist wondered about this bird's habit of constructing nests and conducted a study.
The question was whether the habit of making a nest is learned from mother birds or it is instinct given by Deity.

In the experiment, the researcher did not give this bird grass and leaves, so the bird had to lay eggs without grass and leaves. The eggs hatched and the babies grew up. At this time again, they were not given grass and leaves as well and laid eggs. The five generations passed in the same way.

After the five generations, the researcher gave grass and leaves to birds at their breeding season. What do you think happened? They got the grass and leaves and made a nest with them. The biologist researcher came to the conclusion that birds' innate knowledge of construction of their houses is instinct given by God.

Chapter 10

The Seventh Day of Creation
God's Rest and the Sabbath Day

Reading

"Thus the heavens and the earth were completed, and all their hosts. By the seventh day God completed His work which He had done, and He rested on the seventh day from all His work which He had done. Then God blessed the seventh day and sanctified it, because in it He rested from all His work which God had created and made" (Genesis 2:1-3).

More on the Word

"Remember the sabbath day, to keep it holy" (Exodus 20:8).

"You should brush your teeth after eating."

"You can't eat only what you want."

Our parents tell us what we should do.
They want us to be healthy
and behave well because they love us.

In the same manner, God tells us to keep the Sabbath day.
He does not mean to give us a hard time.
He wants to bless us because He loves us.

1 After the Six Days of the Creation, God Rested on the Seventh Day

After the six days of the Creation, God rested on the earth on the seventh day. He was satisfied seeing the heavens, the earth, and all things in them that He had created with all His heart and devotion. He was pleased and rejoiced thinking about the innumerable true children that He would gain through human cultivation.

God rested, and blessed the seventh day and sanctified it.

2 Keep the Sabbath Holy. It Is the Evidence of Faith!

To keep the Sabbath is the minimum that you can do to show your faith as God's child, and it demonstrates that you believe it was God who finished the work of the six-day Creation and rested on the seventh day.

Ezekiel 20:20 reads, "Sanctify My sabbaths; and they shall be a sign between Me and you, that you may know that I am the LORD your God." As said, to keep the Sabbath holy is the evidence of our faith and it is also related to salvation.

3. Why Did Sunday Become the Sabbath in the New Testament Time?

If you look at most calendars, the first day of the week is Sunday. God the Creator started the works of the Creation on Sunday by saying "Let there be light." On the sixth day, which is Friday, He created land animals and human beings and on the seventh day which is Saturday He rested. In the Old Testament days, Saturday was the Sabbath.

Today, unlike the Old Testament times, Sunday is the Sabbath. What is the reason? This is because it was on Sunday that Jesus, who had died on the wooden cross to redeem us from sins, overcame death and resurrected. The resurrected Lord gave all mankind the hope of resurrection and true rest.

In Matthew 12:8, Jesus referred to Himself as "For the Son of Man is Lord of Sabbath". That is why Christians acknowledge Sunday as the Lord's Day and keep it as the Sabbath in celebration of the resurrection of the Lord.

4. How to Keep the Lord's Day Holy

On the seventh day, God laughed with joy, and His laughter was big enough to shake all the heavens and the earth. Upon seeing Him, the angels praised Him with beautiful songs and performances with instruments.

On the Lord's Day, God's children must not engage themselves in worldly activities. They should not watch worldly TV programs, watch or play sports or participate in recreational games. They must not do evil things like fighting or arguing. They should keep their hearts and thoughts not to do such things.

The Lord's Day is when we go to the church which is the body of the Lord and have true rest in the Lord offering up worship services to God. Thus, we should prepare for the Sunday worship services with our body, heart, mind, and devotion during the week and pray to keep it holy. As it is said that "God blessed the seventh day and sanctified it," if we remember and keep the Lord's Day holy, God will bless us. He will protect us from all accidents and diseases and care for our every affair. Thus, we can have true joy and peace (Isaiah 56:4-7). And we will be able to obtain perfect salvation and enjoy true peace forever in the beautiful Heaven. How blessed it is!

Therefore, on the Lord's Day, we should offer up heartfelt praise to God who gives us beautiful Heaven and thanks to the Lord who opened the way of salvation by His grace.

1. Why should we keep the Sabbath? Fill in the circles.

   To keep the Sabbath is the minimal way to show your faith

   in ◯◯◯ the Creator and it is also related to

   ◯◯◯◯◯◯◯◯◯.

2. Draw lines to connect each of the following to its match.

   | The Sabbath of the Old Testament time | • Sunday • | • The day God rested on the 7th day after the six-day Creation |
   | The Sabbath of the New Testament time | • Saturday • | • The day Jesus was resurrected |

3. Which one keeps the Sabbath appropriately?

   ❶ A child attends Sunday Morning and Evening Services but plays computer games after the services.
   ❷ A child is forced to attend Sunday Services.
   ❸ A child attends the services on GCN when it is cold outside.
   ❹ A child keeps the message delivered in the services in mind with "Amen".

4. Check your Sabbath. Do you keep it holy?

Checkpoints	O	△	X
I do not watch TV or play sports or games on Sunday.			
I do not fight or argue with anyone on Sunday.			
I listen attentively to the message during the service with "Amen".			
Even after Sunday services, I keep my heart holy.			

Mystery of Creation

Plants with Self-protecting Ability!

God gave all living creatures abilities to protect themselves. It was the same for plants that cannot move. There is a plant called "mimosa". When touched, it folds its leaves to protect itself.

Even when touched lightly, it folds its small leaves. When a locust sits on its leaf to eat it, it folds the leaf so that the locust cannot eat its leaf.

Another example is the leaves of a passion flower that are good food for a certain butterfly caterpillar. On the parts of the leaf of a passion

flower are spots that look like the eggs of the butterfly. When a butterfly sees the spots, it is confused in thinking that the leaf already has eggs on it and it flies away.

With this self-protecting ability, they can flourish even when parts of them are eaten by caterpillars. Such abilities enable plants to flourish.

Creatures' Homing Instinct to Find Their Home after Traveling Thousands of Kilometers

The homing instinct is the inherent ability of an animal to navigate towards its home territory, or its breeding area.
Swallows are migratory birds that come to Korea for the summer, and they leave in fall before winter.
On the other hand, wild geese migrate south to Korea when it is winter and go back north when it is summer.

Such migratory birds fly thousands of kilometers exactly towards their destination by instinct.

There are some fish which have this homing instinct. An example of such a fish is the salmon.
Generally, salmon hatches in upper parts of a river and go to the ocean to grow up. Three to six years after they go into the ocean, they are fully grown and swim back to the upper rivers where they were born in order to lay their eggs.

Such amazing instinct of animals is God-given ability.

God the Origin

Before the beginning of time, God existed all by Himself. He was filling up the whole original universe in the form of light that contained sound.

Creation of Spiritual Realm

God, who existed alone for an eternity of years, came to have a thought. He wanted to have another being who could feel the fullness of the things of the universe and who could share love together with Him forever in a beautiful Heaven. To have such true children, He planned 'human cultivation'. So, God the Trinity took on an image, divided the vast universe into four heavens (first, second, third, and fourth heavens), and undertook the work of Creation.

Creation of the Earth

God created the Earth, the place for people to live in the first heaven. He made it with His heart and devotion over an untold period of time. After laying the foundation of the earth with love, He covered it with the water of life. And He let life force permeate the soil of the earth.

Summary of the Creation

★ Seven-day Providence

God the Trinity put on a form that would be the same as that of man, and came down to the earth. What did He do on the earth for 7 days?

The First Day of the Creation

When God said, "Let there be light," the original light of the Creation surrounded the whole universe.

With the light He set the order, principles and natural laws on the earth such as the changing of the day and the night, and through the light the power and divine nature of God would enter into all creatures that would be created.

The Second Day of the Creation

The water of life in which the earth submerged was divided into two when the expanse came to exist between the two. The water under the expanse became the sea of the earth, and the water above the expanse was moved to the second heaven and became the source of the rivers in Eden.

The Third Day of the Creation

The water under the expanse gathered into the North Pole and formed a sea, and in the South Pole, the land was revealed.

God made the vegetation before He made the sun. It was in this way He let us know the fundamental power that can control all things in the universe comes from God.

The Fourth Day of the Creation

The sun, the moon, and stars were created on the fourth day, and the day and the night automatically began to take turns.

On the earth atmospheric and geological phenomena occurred. The earth came to have the four seasons of spring, summer, fall, and winter and the periods of the day and the year were set in motion.

The Fifth Day of the Creation

On the fifth day, the metrological phenomena caused rivers, brooks and streams to be formed on the surface of the earth. Many creatures that lived in the waters and plants in the water, and the birds flying in the sky were also created after their own kind on the fifth day.

The Sixth Day of the Creation

God created and separated 'cattle' from 'wild animals'. Afterwards, He formed the first man Adam from the dust of the ground and breathed into his nostrils the breath of life. The man became a living being.

God planted the Garden of Eden, placed Adam in it and blessed him to live as the lord over all creatures.

The Seventh Day of Rest

After the six-day Creation, God rested on the seventh day. He blessed the day and sanctified it.

All these beautiful things that I am doing

My long-standing hope and desire
Is contained in this man.
Through all these beautiful things that I am doing,
I wish all My hopes and plans
Will be completely fulfilled…

My powerful hands
Touch each part to make organs
And all that is in the body.
Through this man who is made beautifully,
I will be glorified.

Through the son and the son of the sons
My beauty, compassion, meekness,
Fullness of love, and almightiness will be proclaimed.

I make this mouth,
I make the lips, ears, and hands,
Feet and all that is in the body beautifully.

Confession of God the Creator

I am your Father who created you

I have made you people,
And therefore I take responsibility for you
And I guide you.

If you believe in Me and obey Me,
You will see My glory.
You will feel the love of the Father.
I am your Father who created you.

I am Your Father who created you.

 The providence of God the Creator,
who created the first man Adam
with His powerful hands in long-standing hope
and desire and has been taking responsibility
for his descendants and leading them
with expectation
Excerpts from Dr. Jaerock Lee's book *Professions*

We were protected from accidents

Today there are so many car accidents, fire incidents, collapse of buildings, or falling accidents. There are so many accidents occurring even in a day. However, Christians who believe God and live proper believing lives can be protected from all kinds of accidents.

Brother Elijah Kim of Daejeon Manmin Church had a big car accident. While he was driving, his car bumped into a big truck and rolled over. However, he did not hurt at all from head to toe. He gave glory to God.

Brother Anton in Ukraine listened to Dr. Jaerock Lee's sermons with longing and came to lead a diligent Christian life. One day he was protected from a fire incident. A fire  broke out in the shopping mall where his store was located. A hundred fifty shops were burnt but his shop was protected perfectly.

There are many people who were under God's protection even at a dangerous

God is truly alive!

moment that could have claimed their lives. Deacon Kiju Song was working on the construction site to construct a new building. All of a sudden, heavy bundles of wood dropped upon his body.

The shock was so great that he lost balance in his body and he was about to fall to the ground from the fifth floor. People around him felt scared because he could not but just die in that situation.

Right then, a miracle happened. At the moment he fell, he held a steel frame that had been built temporarily. Then, several more bundles of wood dropped to his legs, which rather supported his legs so that he would not fall from the building. He was perfectly protected.

His co-workers witnessed it and even said that God had protected him. They gave glory to God together.

We were protected from disasters

In the Bible, when Elijah prayed, it did not rain for three and a half years. When he prayed for it to rain again, it poured all over the nation (James 5:17-18). When Jesus commanded strong wind and waves to calm down, they calmed down (Mark 4:39).
These works did not just happen in the biblical period, but the same works of control over the weather and metrological phenomena have been occurring through a man of God even today.

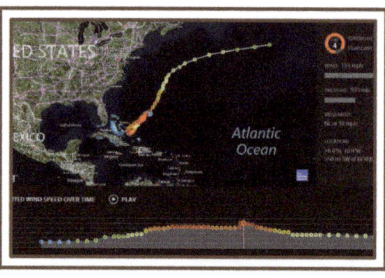

In October, 2015, people in North America were afraid because Hurricane Joaquin was coming to their area. Hurricanes devastate houses and buildings by great downpour and strong wind and waves. They usually cause great damage.

At this critical moment, Pastor Vitaliy Fishberg sent a prayer request to Senior Pastor Dr. Jaerock Lee. Then what do you think happened? The hurricane Joaquin weakened quickly and finally died off.

On April 25, 2015, a major earthquake hit Nepal. This earthquake destroyed many houses and buildings including Hindu temples and claimed many people's lives.

God is truly alive!

In the great disaster, God protected some people. It was Manmin members who lived in Nepal.

When the country was hit by the earthquake, the members of Nepal Manmin Church gathered and prayed  together. And they received Dr. Jaerock Lee's prayer. As a result, its 196 branch and associate churches as well as the church were safely protected. Although their neighbors' houses were all demolished, their houses and their relatives' houses were protected.

In January, 2017, Kenya in Africa was stricken by a severe drought. Many animals died and people were suffering from water   shortage. On January 27, Bishop Dr. Myongho Cheong asked Dr. Jaerock Lee to  pray for the country.

What do you think happened? It rained over almost every part of Kenya for three days from the next day. This news was reported by many media in Kenya.

We were blessed to conceive a baby and for the gender of fetus to change

These days, the number of people who suffer from infertility has been increasing. The conception of a baby is completely in God's works just as Psalm 127:3 reads, "Behold, children are a gift of the LORD." Thus, when they destroy the wall of sins against God and receive the prayer of a powerful pastor, they can fulfill their hearts' desires.

Pastor Suhee Yim was suffering from infertility for 12 years. After she began to attend Manmin Central Church in 2007, however, she gave birth to a healthy boy through Dr. Jaerock Lee's prayer. Besides, many believers came to have a baby after six, seven, or ten years of marriage through his powerful prayer.

God is truly alive!

In 2003, Deaconess Mikyung Lee heard in the hospital that high chances were that she was having a baby with Down syndrome which is chromosomal abnormality. After hearing this, she repented of her past life. Then, she had a dream at night that Dr. Lee appeared. In the dream, he laid his hand on her belly and prayed. As she received the prayer in the dream, her baby's chromosome became normal and she delivered a healthy boy. Hallelujah!

In addition, the power of God the Creator changed male fetus into female or female into male. Twenty two years ago, Senior Deaconess Seonhyo Kim wanted to have a daughter. Unlike her expectation, her baby in her womb was found to be a son. Even at the ninth month of pregnancy, the test revealed it was son. However, she received Dr. Lee's prayer with faith during every worship service. Then, she gave birth to a pretty daughter.

We recovered good eyesight and hearing ability

Once you lose vision or hearing ability, it cannot be recovered with modern medicine. But as Mark 9:23 says, "All things are possible to him who believes," nothing is impossible with the power of God.

Brother Sangyeong Park was diagnosed with brain lesions class IV due to a car accident 23 years ago. He completely lost vision in his left eye. He could not even see light through the eye.

However, during Manmin Summer Retreat 2016, he recovered vision in his left eye after he received Dr. Jaerock Lee's prayer. He came to be able to read letters on calendars through the left eye.

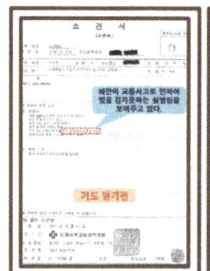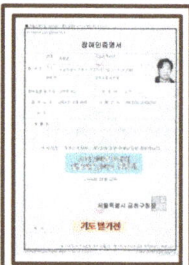

There are also people who recovered hearing ability. Deacon Yongseong Kim is in his seventies. His right eye was blind and he could not hear without hearing aids. His disability was classified as Class 2 Disability. But after he received Dr.

God is truly alive!

Lee's prayer, he experienced amazing works. Light began to enter into his right eye, and he came to distinguish forms of objects. He even came to be able to hear what others are talking about without hearing aids.

In Manmin Summer Retreat, many deaf people have recovered their hearing abilities every year and glorified God.

We were healed of incurable diseases

Despite the rapid development of science and medicine, there are still so many diseases that are hard to treat or impossible to treat. However, the power of God cures countless incurable diseases such as stroke, cerebral palsy, and AIDS. His power heals atopic dermatitis that modern medicine cannot cure completely.

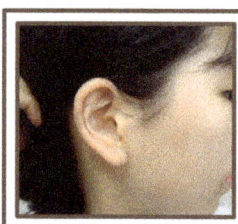

Sister Miri Park was suffering from oozing sores on her face and arm and serious itchiness. She repented that she had loved the world and received Dr. Jaerock Lee's prayer. Not long after it, she was completely healed of it.

Aside from her case, there are so many believers who experienced healing of atopic dermatitis.

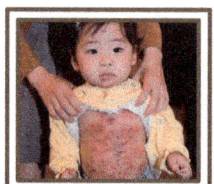 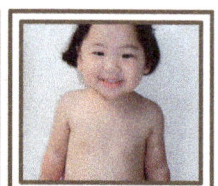

  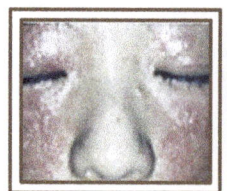 

God is truly alive!

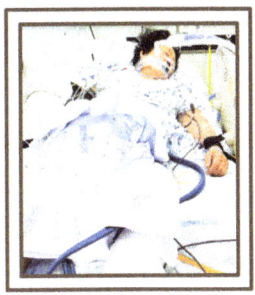 

Deaconess Kyunghwa Yeo collapsed due to acute myocardial infarction. She was moved to emergency room but she did not come around. The doctor said that because twenty minutes passed after her heart had stopped she would not recover consciousness. He added even if she came around she could not live normally because of brain damage. However, after Dr. Lee's prayer for the sick, she regained consciousness and recovered her health quickly. She is now very healthy.

Brother Bampa Sela Omer in DR Congo was inflicted with AIDS for several years. The hospital told him that he would not have many days left to live. But he registered in Kinshasa Manmin Church and asked for the grace of God in worship services and prayer meetings.

Amazingly, God answered his prayer. While he was receiving Dr. Lee's prayer during Manmin Summer Retreat 2015 on GCN, his body became hot and all pains were gone. He recovered good health.

**Dr. Jaerock Lee
Junior Bible Study**

Seven-Day Providence by Dr. Jaerock Lee
Published by Urim Books (Representative: Seongnam Vin)
73, Yeouidaebang-ro 22-gil, Dongjak-gu, Seoul, Korea
www.urimbooks.com

All rights reserved. This book or parts thereof may not be reproduced in any form, stored in a retrieval system, or transmitted in any form or by any means, electronic, mechanical, photocopying, recording or otherwise, without prior written permission of the publisher.

Unless otherwise noted, all Scripture quotations are taken from the Holy Bible, NEW AMERICAN STANDARD BIBLE, ®, Copyright © 1960, 1962, 1963, 1968, 1971, 1972, 1973, 1975, 1977, 1995 by The Lockman Foundation. Used by permission.

Copyright © 2017 by Dr. Jaerock Lee
ISBN: 979-11-263-0312-0 73230
Translation Copyright © 2017 by Dr. Esther K Chung. Used by permission.

First Edition *June 2017*

Previously published in Korean in 2017 by Urim Books in Seoul, Korea

Edited by Dr. Geumsun Vin
Designed by Design Team of Urim Books
Printed by Prione Printing
For more information contact: urimbook@hotmail.com

www.ingramcontent.com/pod-product-compliance
Lightning Source LLC
LaVergne TN
LVHW070527070526
838199LV00073B/6716